THE GRILL COOKBOOK

Perfectly Simple Italian Specialties
for Your Best Grill Parties

Joe Sullivan

Table of Contents

Introduction

Grilling is one of the most original forms of cooking. If the kitchen is moved outside when the outside temperature is pleasant, the dishes prepared in this way taste even better. In addition, there is a very special feeling of being together and preparing food together. Grilling was never really out of fashion, but has experienced a real boom in recent years, which is related to various cookery programs on TV and the large grill manufacturers who keep bringing new devices and products onto the market and thus for an ever-expanding spectrum Provide opportunities and methods.

Grilling

In the original sense, the term "grilling" refers to roasting over an open fire. When grilling, the grilled food is cooked by radiant heat and roasted on the surface. In addition to the roasted substances, this process also creates the aroma typical of grilling.

Which Grill Is The Right One? - Presentation Of The Different Types Of Barbecues

Opinions are divided on this question. There are 100%

supporters of charcoal and equally enthusiastic supporters of modern gas grills. So that you can get a more detailed picture of the various grills and their special technology, we would like to show you to the most important grills:

- charcoal grill

The charcoal grill or charcoal grill is the epitome of the grill for many. Glowing fans of this type of grill are convinced that grilling with charcoal creates a distinctive taste. However, numerous studies show that with the classic preparation process, there is no great difference in taste between the food on the charcoal grill and that on the gas grill. It is, however, the case that when grilling on charcoal, dripping fat or other liquids can fall on the embers, causing additional smoke to settle on the grilled food. This creates a very special taste, but it is not good for your health.

Make sure that no fat drips into the embers when using a charcoal grill.

To refine the barbecue enjoyment when using a charcoal grill, you can add special smoking chips or watered wood shavings (e.g. walnut or fruit woods such as cherry) to the embers. The smoke that you generate in this way is very aromatic, contributes to a special taste and is harmless to health.

A special highlight of the charcoal grill is the smell that arises when grilling with charcoal and does not appear when grilling with gas.

There are numerous versions of charcoal grills in stores: The range on offer ranges from very small disposable grills to inexpensive models in many formats and luxury designs in various sizes.

When purchasing a charcoal grill, it is advisable to make sure that the grill has a lid. A lid is particularly necessary for indirect grilling, as otherwise, the heat cannot be retained.

Well-equipped charcoal grills allow you to use the grill grate at different heights to regulate the heat. Variably adjustable ventilation slots are also very useful in this context. If you let more air into the embers, this means more heat, while restricting the air supply reduces the temperature somewhat. Regardless of the features of the charcoal grill, its temperature can also be controlled via the amount of charcoal used.

- The kettle grill - a special design

Classic kettle grills are designed as charcoal grills. Since this design is now enjoying great popularity, kettle grills are also offered with the gas operation.

The kettle grill was originally invented to prevent the fat from the grill from dripping into the embers and causing them to burn. However, other advantages of this design were soon discovered, such as excellent stability.

Due to its characteristic shape, the kettle grill is ideal for the preparation of many different grilled goods. For example, it is no problem to cook a thick T-bone steak or a whole chicken on this grill.

A kettle grill is usually made up of two hemispheres: The lower part (often with a mobile stand) is used to hold the coals (with a charcoal grill), whereby these are placed on their own grate, which provides additional ventilation from below, whereby the Development of an even heat is possible. The actual grill grate is in a slightly raised position above the charcoal grate. Ball grills are often used in this context for indirect grilling. Accordingly, it is not grilled directly over the coals. First and foremost, the warm air and smoke are used for cooking the food to be grilled. The top part of the kettle grill is the lid. This can also be provided with additional practical equipment such as a thermometer or adjustable ventilation openings.

Ball grills can, of course, not only be used for the indirect grilling process but also for grilling directly over the embers.

- Gas grill - grilling with gas

Gas grills generate hot air, which is then used for grilling. One of the advantages of gas grills is that they are very easy to light and very easy to regulate. In addition, the desired temperature can be reached fairly quickly with the gas grill, which saves time compared to the charcoal grill.

Gas bottles for operating such grills are available in various sizes in stores and are easy to get, which is why frequent grill use is not a problem at all. For unadulterated barbecue enjoyment and for the greatest possible flexibility and spontaneity, it is advisable to always have a filled replacement bottle in the house.

Gas grills are built in different ways: There are grills that use lava stones or ceramic briquettes. These are quickly heated up by the burning gas and then transfer to the heat to the food to be grilled. In addition, the lava stones or ceramic briquettes also catch the dripping fat. In other model variants of this grill type, the gas flames heat rods made of special steel or cast iron, which are located under the actual grill grate, which absorbs and release the heat.

Gas barbecues are usually equipped with two or, ideally, even more burners, which allow good control over where in the grill a particularly large amount of direct heat should be available.

Most grills that run on gas are usually very generous in size so that four to six people can be supplied with delicious grill specialities at the same time without any problems. In addition, there are of course also models with a particularly large grill area, which is ideal for parties and other events, as well as very space-saving variants that are easy to transport and, for example, provide good service on the campsite.

Almost all gas grills are equipped with lids. When closed, they keep the heat very well and also offer a wide range of uses.

- Table Grill / Electric Grill

The table grill or electric grill can also be used without any problems within the apartment, regardless of the weather and season. You only need a socket for its operation. Another advantage of the table grill / electric grill is that no smoke is generated when it is used so that the neighbours are not disturbed when used outside on the balcony.

Table grills / electric grills are usually only suitable for indirect grilling to a limited extent so that traditional direct grilling is used here.

In terms of size, most table grills / electric grills are rather short, so that larger groups of people can only be supplied with a single device with great difficulty. For this reason, it is our recommendation for rainy days and a small number of people.

- Dutch oven

The Dutch Oven is not an everyday grill device, which is wonderful as a second device or additional grill. It is a cast-iron pot with a lid. Usually, the pot is placed on a suitable stand, which stands directly in glowing coals. In addition, glowing coals are placed on the lid of the Dutch Oven. In this way, heat is evenly transferred to the food placed in the pot so that it is prepared gently, and all of the aromatic substances are retained.

The Dutch Oven gets very hot when it is used, which is why it must be handled with care. In this context, the trade offers Dutch Oven grill sets which, in addition to one or more pots in different sizes, also include useful accessories such as a lid lifter.

Due to its nature and use, the Dutch Oven is ideal for indirect grilling. How many people can be "fed up" with it depends, among other things, on its size and the grilled food used.

What Grill Methods Are There?

If you deal with the topic of grilling, you will almost automatically be confronted with the terms direct grilling and indirect grilling. There are differences between the two grill methods; explain the advantages and disadvantages and give you a lot of additional information.

- Direct grilling

The direct grilling method is the classic method of grilling. Here the grilled food is cooked in a short time at high temperatures from approx. 250 ° C. Depending on the kind technology used, the distance between the food to be grilled and the heat source is adjusted as required. When grilling directly, the typical brown crust is created on the food.

Since the direct grilling process "works" at high temperatures, the cooking times are short.

Basically, all grilled food with a cooking time of <30 minutes is suitable for direct grilling. This includes, for example, steaks in any shape, chops, sausages, skewers and various vegetables.

You should rather refrain from deglazing with beer, as this process creates additional smoke or soot, which is deposited on the grilled food, which is said to be hazardous to health.

Depending on the nature of the grillage, the heat generated by the direct grilling process creates a deliberate "drawing" on the meat surface. This is also known as branding. The best results can be achieved in this context with cast iron grills, as these distribute the heat extremely evenly.

- Indirect grilling

For example, indirect grilling is often used when using a kettle grill. With this method, the food is not positioned directly over the charcoal. Instead, the heat acts equally on meat, vegetables, etc., from all sides.

For indirect grilling, a bowl filled with water is placed under the food to be grilled. It serves to catch the dripping fat. In this way, the humidity in the closed grill is significantly higher, which means that meat, for example, is tender and juicy. If you want to influence the taste of indirect grilling, you can also fill the fat drip tray with wine or beer instead of water.

Gas grills are also suitable for indirect grilling: the gas grill is preheated before the food is placed on the grill. If you put meat, fish and Co. on the grill, you switch off the burners, which are located directly below. The lid of the gas grill is then kept closed for indirect grilling, as when using a kettle grill or similar charcoal grill model.

What Care Does The Grill Need?

If you do not need the grill, you should always store it in a dry place, regardless of its type. It does not matter whether you place a coal or gas grill in a garden shed, tool shed, in the basement or in a storage room. If there is no such space available, you should at least get a suitable protective cover or cover that protects the grill from the elements.

When grilling, juice and fat come out of the grilled food, ash and residues are formed, and leftovers stick to the grillage. Cleaning the grill is therefore essential for long-term barbecuing pleasure. In the Wohnen.de magazine, we explain what you should look out for when using charcoal barbecues, gas barbecues and when cleaning the grill grate:

- Clean and maintain the charcoal grill

After using a charcoal grill, all residues such as the cold ash and the cooled charcoal must be disposed of. Make sure that there really is nothing left to glow. To be on the safe side, you can wait until the next day. Then, sweep the charcoal area of the grill with an old broom or hand brush.

- Clean and care for the gas grill

When grilling on the gas grill, the gas supply must, of course, be turned off. After the gas grill has cooled down, empty the drip trays for the fat and wash them out with hot water and a splash of detergent. Use a damp cloth to clean the grill bars. Remove any food particles that have fallen down. Also, check to see if the torch or nozzles are clogged. If there is a blockage, thorough cleaning is also advisable here. After cleaning the gas grill with a damp cloth, you should reheat it briefly afterwards so that any moisture that may have remained evaporates and rust cannot form.

If your gas grill has lava stones, you can boil them in vinegar water once or twice a year to remove fat and other residues.

- Clean and care for the grill grate

The grill grate is the most stressed when grilling. Usually, after grilling, some food and fat residues adhere to the grate and have to be removed. If you want to clean the grate when it is cold, this is not really an easy job. Ideally, you should dedicate yourself to cleaning the grate immediately after grilling. Take the grate off the fire while it is still warm. Use the grill tongs to grab a cloth soaked in oil and rub it firmly over the grillage. With the oil, you not only lay the foundation for optimal grilling results the next time you use it but also protect it from corrosion.

Grilled prawns skewers

Ingredients

tbsp Olive oil

Parsley

Ground garlic

24 Prawns

1 glass

Breadcrumbs

Preparation

Total time: 20 mins

Preparation: 15 mins

Cooking: 5 min

STEP 1

Shell the prawns and put them in a salad bowl. Pour a little olive oil and mix with a spoon.

STEP 2

Sprinkle with ground garlic and parsley to taste. Mix again.

STEP 3

Then pour the glass of breadcrumbs over the prawns and mix everything together, taking care to coat the prawns well. Increase the amounts of ingredients if necessary.

STEP 4

Then thread the prawns one by one on a skewer, preferably metal.

STEP 5

Cook on the barbecue over the coals until the prawns turn a nice orange-pink color.

STEP 6

Serve with a mixed salad or rice with a hot pepper fondue.

Random recipe

25 mins

Ingredients

Salt

Pepper

Olive oil

Cayenne pepper

Provence herbs

2 pods Garlic

1 Courgette

2 Shallots

Preparation

Total time: 25 mins

Preparation: 10 minutes

Cooking: 15 mins

STEP 1

Coarsely peel the zucchini, keeping a little zucchini skin and cut fairly thin slices lengthwise that you have in a container going in the fridge.

STEP 2

Add the minced garlic and shallot and the spices (possibility to vary the spices!)

STEP 3

Add olive oil so that the zucchini slices bathe well in the marinade.

STEP 4

Marinate in the refrigerator for at least 6 hours (can marinate more than 24 hours without problem, so you can make the leftovers the next day!)

STEP 5

Place an aluminum foil with raised edges on the barbecue grill, and arrange the marinated zucchini slices next to each other.

STEP 6

Turn the slices halfway through cooking or when the zucchini begins to grill.

STEP 7

Cooking is done when the slices have softened and are lightly toasted.

STEP 8

A delight to accompany grilled meats, ideal in summer!

STEP 9

Have a good meal!

Tender meat in the oven

Ingredients FOR 5 SERVINGS

Pork ham 700 gr

Red wine 100 ml

garlic 2 of tooth.

soy 1

Dry spices 1

salt 1

Preparation

time: 2 p.m.

Prepare the ingredients. To cook tender meat in the oven we will need: a piece of pork (ham, carbonade), soy sauce, table wine, garlic, spices for pork and salt.

Wash the pork ham, dry with paper towels. Grate the meat with salt and spices for meat.

Peel the garlic and cut into petals.

In meat make a knife deep punctures. Stuff the meat with garlic petals.

Put the meat in a bowl, grease with soy sauce, trying to make the sauce into the incisions.

Tighten the bowl with food wrap and refrigerate for 12 hours. Marinated meat to be tied with a culinary thread so that it does not lose shape and put in a deep baking dish.

Drizzle the meat with red wine.

Cover the shape with foil and press the edges well. Bake the meat for 30 minutes at 220 degrees Celsius, then another 45 minutes at 180 degrees Celsius.

Remove the ham from the oven, cool and cut into slices.

Enjoy your meal!

Zucchini dips (for grill or barbecue)

40 mins

Ingredients

Utensils 10

50 g Crushed almonds

75 g Sugar

100 ml Wine vinegar (white)

300 g Courgette

5 Kiwi fruit

1/2 teaspoon

Cayenne pepper

Preparation

Total time: 40 mins

Preparation: 10 minutes

Cooking: 30 mins

STEP 1

Clean, cut the kiwis, zucchini into small cubes and put them in a saucepan.

STEP 2

Add salt, pepper, vinegar and almonds.

STEP 3

Mix well, bring to the boil, then cook over low heat for about 30 minutes.

Pork peritoneum roll in the oven

Ingredients for 12 servings

Pork 2 kg

Mustard ready2

Soy2

Salt3

White pepper1 gr.ch.

Nutmeg1 gr.ch.

Garlic powder1

Preparation

time: 2 hours 20 mins

How to make a roll of pork peritoneum in the oven? Prepare the right products. Defrost the meat in advance. A set of spices can use your own, if desired. Any ready-made dry mix of seasonings for meat in the oven will be suitable. Garlic powder can be replaced with garlic cloves. White pepper can also be replaced with red or black ground. Or use a mixture of peppers.

Clean the pork peritoneum from all excess. I cut her skin off, cut the bones. Wash the meat thoroughly and dry it with paper towels.

My pig's belly looks like this after cleaning. That is, it is so thin that it is easy to roll into a roll.

If you have fresh garlic, peel and grind it in any way you can conveniently. In a separate bowl, combine the finished mustard, salt, nutmeg, white pepper, garlic powder (or crushed garlic) and soy sauce. It's marinade. Make incisions on the meat. And rinse the pork well with the cooked marinade.

Turn the meat over to the other side and smear it with marinade on this side too. At this stage, you can add fresh chopped greens, making it a filling for the roll. I cooked without greens.

Twist the pork into a tight roll.

Tie the roll with twine as shown in the photo. This will help the roll not to fall apart during the baking process and to keep the desired shape.

Wrap the roll in foil. In this form, let him lie down for about half an hour. Then transfer the roll in foil to a baking dish or on a baking tray. And place in a preheated oven to 200C to bake for about 2 hours. Determine the exact time and temperature of the roasting by your oven. The weight of meat also affects it. Mine weighs 2 kilos.

10 minutes before the end of baking open the foil and continue to bake the meat. You can hold it in the oven for a little longer until the roll is browned. Check the meat's readiness so: pierce it with a sharp knife in the middle. If the juice comes out light, then it is ready! Enjoy your meal!

Note that the quality and taste of the finished dish depends on the proper defrosting of the ingredients. How to avoid mistakes and choose the best way, read in the article about defrost.

When adding soy sauce to a dish it is worth considering that it has a rather salty taste. Reduce the total amount of salt, otherwise you run the risk of oversalting.

Keep in mind that the ovens are different for everyone. The temperature and cooking time may differ from those mentioned in the recipe. To make any baked dish successful.

Roasted cockerels or pigeons in the oven

40 mins

Ingredients

2 pods

Garlic

Rosemary

Thyme

Pepper

Salt

2 Cockerels or pigeons

2 teaspoons

Melted butter

Preparation

Total time: 40 mins

Preparation: 10 minutes

Cooking: 30 mins

STEP 1

Wash the pigeons, cut them with shears.

STEP 2

Mix the ingredients with the crushed garlic and melted butter.

STEP 3

Brush the poultry halves.

STEP 4

Place them in a baking dish.

STEP 5

Bake for 30 minutes at 220 ° C (thermostat 7-8), basting regularly. Turn halfway through cooking.

Grilled cheese sandwich

6 min

Ingredients

2 slices

Sandwich bread (white and very soft, English style)

1 slice Gruyere

Butter

Preparation

Total time: 6 min

Preparation: 1 min

Cooking: 5 min

STEP 1

Assemble the croque: 1 slice of bread, 1 slice of cheese, 1 slice of bread.

STEP 2

Heat up a knob of butter inside the pan.

STEP 3

Place the croque in the pan (soak in butter on both sides).

STEP 4

Cook over medium-high heat till both sides are golden brown and cheese is melted.

STEP 5

Cut into a triangle!

Grilled eggplant withchermoula

40 mins

Ingredients

Coarse salt

Olive oil

2 Eggplants

For the chermoula:

Cayenne pepper (optional)

Salt

Pepper

1 teaspoon

Ground cinnamon

1 tbsp Ground cumin

3 tbsp Chopped fresh cilantro

2 pods Crushed garlic

6 cl Lemon juice green

Preparation

Total time: 40 mins

Preparation: 30 mins

Cooking: 10 minutes

STEP 1

Cut eggplants in slices 1 cm thick then let them drain for 20 minutes with coarse salt.

STEP 2

Rinse thoroughly and dry with absorbent paper then brush them with olive oil.

STEP 3

Grill on the oven grill for about 5 minutes on each side then drain them on paper towels.

STEP 4

Reserve.

STEP 5

Mix all the ingredients necessary for the preparation of the chermoula.

STEP 6

Combine the eggplant slices and chermoula in a bowl.

STEP 7

To be enjoyed warm with grilled meat or fish or cold in a salad.

Pumpkin soup with bacon and grilled hazelnuts

50 mins

Ingredients

1 liter Water

Olive oil

30 g Shelled hazelnuts

Bacon (proportion to choose according to taste)

2 Chicken stock cubes

1 kg Pumpkin

20 cl Sour cream

1 Onion

Preparation

Total time: 50 mins

Preparation: 20 mins

Cooking: 30 mins

STEP 1

Peel the onion and brown it in olive oil then add the peeled pumpkin and cut into large cubes. Sauté well then pour the liter of water into the casserole dish.

STEP 2

Add the two chicken cubes in the casserole dish then cook for 30 minutes over medium heat, covered.

STEP 3

Once cooked, add the crème fraîche and mix to obtain a velvety.

STEP 4

Toast the hazelnuts on a very hot pan and add them to the velouté.

STEP 5

Also grill the bacon in the same hot pan and add to the velouté.

STEP 6

It's ready!

Grilled shoulder of lamb with spices and honey

Ingredients

Salt

Pepper

Olive oil

1 beautiful branch

Tomato (clusters) (optional)

1 kg Potato (optional)

2 Olive oil

Half Lemon

1 dose Saffron

1 half Sweet pepper

1 half Cinnamon

1 teaspoon Cumin

3 Ginger

Preparation

Total time: 1h10

Preparation: 15 mins

Cooking: 55 mins

Wash the potatoes and cook them for 10 minutes in plenty of salted water.

Preheat the oven to 200 ° (thermostat 6/7).

Mix with all the spices, ginger (peeled, cut into small pieces), lemon juice, olive oil and a little pepper (DO NOT USE HONEY YET).

Brush the shoulder with this mixture and let marinate if you have time otherwise cook it right away.

Place the shoulder inside a large baking dish, surround the lightly cooked potatoes and the branch of tomatoes.

Drizzle the vegetables with olive oil then salt and pepper them.

Put in the oven for 30 minutes.

Take out the dish, turn the potatoes a little and sprinkle the meat with the honey. Also pour a small glass of water in the bottom of the dish. Return to the oven for 10 to 15 minutes for cooking <>.

Let the meat rest a little before serving it sliced, along with the vegetables and the sauce that you can collect from the bottom of the dish.

Grilled summer vegetables

30 mins

Ingredients

Salt

Pepper

Olive oil

5 pods

Garlic

3 Peppers

2 Eggplants

2 Zucchini

1 Onions

Chopped fresh basil (or, failing that, dried)

Preparation

Total time: 30 mins

Preparation: 5 min

Cooking: 25 mins

Cut zucchini to 1 cm thick slices, leaving the skin on, the eggplant in half-slices of 1/2 cm, the onions in quarters and the peppers in large pieces.

Place the vegetables on an oiled baking sheet and drizzle with olive oil. Season with salt and then pepper and sprinkle with grated garlic and chopped basil.

Mix and repeat the operation if necessary. Place in a preheated oven, + grill position at 240 ° C (thermostat 8). Turn the vegetables during cooking so that they grill evenly. The cooking time depends on the oven, I take them out when they have browned a little.

Grilled vegetables

Ingredients

1 red pepper

400g Enringi Mushrooms

1 courgette

1 eggplant

50 ml olive oil

1 tsp adjiki dry

Preparation

Cut into large pieces.

Marinate in oil and spices.

Fry on the grill.

Pork chop with grilled vegetables with rosemary

Ingredients

1 serving

1 pork loin on the bone

4 medium mushrooms

1 sprig of rosemary

2 cloves garlic

1 little courgette

1 small onion

4 cherry

salt, pepper

20g butter

Preparation

Melt the oil in a frying pan, add rosemary, crushed garlic. Fry until the garlic is golden.

Fry the pork in this oil, periodically pouring steak. (ready to identify by juice).

Vegetables cut plates, fry on the grill or a regular frying pan, grease with oil for flavor.

Put on a plate, decorate and serve hot.

Warm salad with grilled vegetables and goat cheese

20 mins

Ingredients 4 servings

2 pieces of paprika (yellow or orange)

1 piece Courgette

400g Spinach (baby)

400g Field Salad

50g Goat cheese

For refueling:

1 tbsp Olive oil

1/2 tsp balsamic vinegar

1 tbsp honey

to taste Salt, pepper

Preparation

Cut the courgettes into rings and paprika into longitudinal pieces. Grease the vegetables with olive oil and bake on the grill or barbecue.

For dressing, mix honey, olive oil and balsamic vinegar, season to taste.

Mix vegetables with lettuce and spinach. Put the pieces of cheese on top and pour the dressing.

Grilled vegetables

30 minutes

Ingredients

6 people

2 pieces Pepper Bulgarian

2 pieces Aubergine

3 pieces Tomato

1 piece zucchini courgette

Black ground pepper

pinch salt

3 tbsp olive oil

3-4 clove Garlic

Preparation

Wash the vegetables, cut into medium size.

Fry on a preheated grill alternately, tomatoes last.

Put on a dish, pepper and add squeezed garlic and olive oil, a pleasant appetite!

Snack to grilled vegetablekebabs

40 minutes

Ingredients

25 servings

5 aubergine

5 Zucchini

5 Bulgarian pepper

marinade:

150 grams. vegetable oil

3 tbsp. soy sauce

1 tbsp. hops-suneli

2 cloves garlic

Preparation

Eggplant cut in circles, it is better to thicken about 2 cm.

From the Bulgarian remove the core and cut into 4-6 pieces.
Depends on the size of the pepper.

You don't have to clean the zucchini, just cut it down into several pieces.

Stir all the vegetables in a deep bowl.

Prepare the marinade for vegetables. Mix vegetable oil and soy sauce, squeezed garlic, suneli hops. stir.

Add the marinade to the vegetables, evenly mix over all the

vegetables.

Leave for 15-20 minutes. Let the vegetables soak.

If desired, you can add tomatoes, they immediately put on the grill. Put the vegetables on a grill and grill for 5 minutes on each side.

Grilled vegetables to serve warm. Enjoy your meal! You can serve to vegetables sour cream and garlic sauce.

Fine Grilled vegetables

Ingredients

cauliflower

carrot

zucchini

Salt, pepper, spices

vegetable oil

Preparation

Colored cabbage to disassemble into inflorescences, chop carrots and zucchini. Send the cabbage and carrots to boiling, salted water for 2-3 minutes. Drain the water, leave the vegetables under the lid.

Salt, pepper, season with spices (I have ground rosemary). Add the butter, cabbage and carrots, stir. Put on a preheated grill pan, bring to readiness. Enjoy your meal!

Fresh Grilled vegetables

Ingredients

4 servings

2-3 pieces of courgettes

2 pieces eggplant

3-4 pieces Carrots

0.5 kg Mushrooms mushrooms

Spices, salt

oil

Preparation

Cut the vegetables into circles of 0.5 cm.

Salt, add pepper, smoked paprika, garlic, vegetable oil.

Fry on the grills, it is better after the meat, when the heat subsides for 4-5 minutes on each side.

Mediterranean grilledvegetables

50 mins and 1 hour of marinating

Ingredients

4 servings

1 piece Courgette

1 piece Aubergine

2 pieces Red sweet paprika

2 cloves Garlic

8 tbsp Olive oil

1 tbsp "Italian herbs" seasoning

2 tbsp capers

50g Pine nuts

20g Parsley

to taste Salt, pepper

Preparation

Paprika cut in half and remove the seeds. Bake in the oven for 15-20 minutes. Put the closed dishes and leave under the lid for 20 minutes.

Cut courgettes and eggplant into rings and grill.

Squeeze the garlic through the press and mix with the olive oil and spices.

Put the courgettes and eggplants on a wide dish on top of put the paprika. Drizzle the vegetables with dressing and sprinkle with capers, pine nuts and chopped greens. Leave the vegetables at least an hour to infuse at room temperature.

Lamb ribs with vegetables

Ingredients

6 servings

1.5 kg of lamb ribs

2 Onion

50 ml vegetable oil (for roasting ribs)

salt

2 packets of grilled vegetables

dry seasoning for lamb

100ml water

Preparation

Fry the lamb ribs until blush.

Cut the onions in large pieces. Transfer the ribs to a thick-walled pan. Fill the ribs with onions, pour water and simmer under the lid for 1.5 hours.

After half an hour, add vegetables and lamb seasoning to the ribs. Salt and simmer for another half an hour.

Serve the finished dish on the table. Fresh or pickled vegetables can be served to lamb ribs. Enjoy your meal!

Grilled vegetables with friedfish and homemade sauce

45 minutes

Ingredients

3 servings

2 medium zucchini

2 Bulgarian peppers

500g mint fillet

spices

olive oil

red onion

sour cream, mustard, mayonnaise

greens

Preparation

Cut the fillet into small pieces, season (a mixture for fish dishes), fry in olive oil.

Vegetables chop, fold in a deep bowl, add olive oil q lemon juice mix seasonings for grilled vegetables, bowl shake well (mix).

On a well-heated with olive oil grilled pan fry all vegetables on both sides.

Cooking sauce - in a bowl mix sour cream, a little mayonnaise and mustard, green onion and dill, spices.

Put the fish, vegetables and sauce on a plate. A healthy and delicious dinner is ready. Enjoy your meal!

Aubergine - Tomate

Ingredients

1 eggplant

2 medium tomatoes

1 head of mozzarella cheese

1 tbsp olive oil

to taste Salt and pepper

For the sauce

1 tsp seasoning for grilled vegetables

1 tbsp olive oil

Preparation

Rinse and dry the eggplant, cut the cutting. Cut into plates along from the cutting and spread the fan pressing to do so on the cutting. Salt, pepper.

Cut the tomatoes and cheese into rounds and put on a plate of eggplant.

For the sauce, mix the seasoning and olive oil and pour this mixture of eggplant on top, sprinkle with Provence herbs.

Bake in the oven at 180 degrees for 20 minutes.

Everyone's in a great mood.

Homemade Wok pasta withcrispy grilled vegetables for dinner

Ingredients

4 servings

1 piece zucchini

1 piece of tomato

1 onion

1 piece of Bulgarian pepper

Lemon (for sauce)

soy

5 cloves Garlic (not too small)

150 grams of Spaghetti Pasta zara or Maltagliati in dry form

Vegetable oil for roasting

50g Kinza

Preparation

1. Boil the spaghetti, throw it on a colander and leave for a while.

2. Shiny onions in half rings.

3. Cut the tomato into cubes.

4. Cut into slices of pepper.

5. Tsukini clean from the skin, and cut into cubes.

6. On a hot pan (I have a grill) greased with vegetable oil put

onions and fry until slightly golden (the main thing is to stir quickly and do not move away otherwise risk to burn).

7. Remove the onion in a bowl, and fry the zucchini cubes, remove to the onion.

8. Fry the bell pepper, stirring quickly, then proceed to the tomato.

9. Combine all products and mix.

Grilled sweet potatoes

25 mins

Ingredients

Freshly ground pepper

Flower of salt

2 Sweet potatoes

50 g Melted butter

Preparation

Total time: 25 mins

Preparation: 15 mins

Cooking: 10 minutes

STEP 1

Peel the potatoes, cut them into slices 2 cm thick.

STEP 2

Brush each round with melted butter,

STEP 3

sprinkle the fleur de sel and pepper on each ring.

STEP 4

Place the rings on the oven rack. Turn on the oven (grill position) and put in the oven as soon as the grill is red.

STEP 5

Cook for 4 to 5 minutes.

STEP 6

Take out the potatoes, do the same on the other side of the slices.

Nadine's salted bacon andgrilled hazelnut muffins

25 mins

Ingredients

For the dry mix:

1 level teaspoon

Fine salt

1/2 bag Yeast

2 teaspoons Baking soda (optional)

225 g Flour

For the wet mix:

2 cl Milk

2 Eggs

80 g Melted butter

1 Natural yogurt

For garnish:

200 g Bacon

50 g Hazelnut

Preparation

Total time: 25 mins

Preparation: 5 min

Cooking: 20 mins

STEP 1

Cut the bacon into small pieces and very coarsely crush the hazelnuts (roughly, cut them in 2 or 3). Grill together in a pan (no fat) and let cool.

STEP 2

In a bowl, mix all ingredients for the dry mixture.

STEP 3

In a second bowl, break the eggs and beat them a little, add the melted butter, yogurt and milk. Mix well. This base can be used for all savory muffins.

STEP 4

Add the contents of the pan, including the fat, and mix well.

STEP 5

Suddenly pour the dry mixture into the wet mixture and mix very little with a spoon (lumps remain, this is normal).

STEP 6

Fill the muffin tins (greased if they are not silicone) to 3/4 and bake 20 minutes Th 6-7 (190 ° C).

STEP 7

Serve it well chilled, either as an aperitif or as a starter.

Vegetables - grilled

Ingredients

0.5 kg Mushrooms mushrooms

2 pieces Pepper Bulgarian

2 pieces eggplant

2 pieces of courgettes

Vegetable oil

grilling seasoning

garlic, soy sauce

Provence herbs

Preparation

Marinate mushrooms in soy sauce for half an hour and fry in a grill pan.

Cut the vegetables and fry too.

Fold all the vegetables on a baking tray, sprinkle with seasonings for grilling and Provence herbs, sprinkle with crushed garlic, sprinkle with soy sauce and vegetable oil.

Put in a preheated 200g oven for 10 minutes.

Grilled bars with pastis andfennel

35 mins

Ingredients

Salt

Pepper

2 Lemons

2 tbsp Pastis

5 tbsp Olive oil

700 g bars emptied

2 bulbs Fennel

Preparation

Total time: 35 mins

Preparation: 15 mins

Cooking: 20 mins

STEP 1

Preheat oven to 210 ° C (thermostat 7).

STEP 2

Mix the pastis and the oil. Chop the fennels finely.

STEP 3

Cut the fish with 2-3 notches on each side, brush the inside with the pastis mixture, salt and pepper. Garnish with fennel and place in a large baking dish. Pour the rest of the pastis oil in the bottom of the dish and over the fish, and add 1/2 glass of water.

STEP 4

Bake for 20 minutes in the oven, sprinkling with lemon juice from time to time.

Grilled peppers in oil

35 mins

Ingredients

Salt

Pepper

20 cl Olive oil

1 clove Garlic

2 Red peppers

2 Yellow peppers

Preparation

Total time: 35 mins

Preparation: 15 mins

Cooking: 20 mins

STEP 1

Wash and grill the peppers for 20 minutes under the oven grill, turning them often.

STEP 2

Put them in a plastic bag and let cool to peel them more easily.

STEP 3

Then peel them and seed them. Cut them into strips.

STEP 4

Salt, pepper, sprinkle with garlic, chop and sprinkle with olive oil.

STEP 5

Reserve in the fridge.

Grilled vegetable salad with chicken

Ingredients

2 pieces of chicken fillet

2 pieces of Bulgarian pepper

1 piece zucchini

1 eggplant

1 fresh cucumber

greens

Salt, pepper

Vegetable oil

1-2 cloves garlic

Preparation

Grill the chicken breast.

Vegetables are also grilled (peppers, zucchini, eggplant). Eggplant pre-cut into large rings, salt, leave for 10 minutes, then rinse from salt, dry with a paper towel and just fry on the grill.

All cool and cut into strips.

Fresh cucumber is also cut into strips.

Cut the chicken fillet into strips.

All mix, add salt, pepper to taste, chopped greens, vegetable oil, garlic through press. Stir.

Vegetables - grilled in Spanishwith mint vinaigrette dressing

30 mins

Ingredients 4 servings

2 pieces of red paprika

2 pieces Courgette green

1 piece Courgette yellow

2 pieces Aubergine

2 handful Cherry Tomatoes

2-3 tbsp olive oil

For refueling:

5 tbsp olive oil

1 tbsp red wine vinegar

1/2 tbsp Lemon juice

2 cloves Garlic

3 sprigs of mint

Salt, pepper

Preparation

BB'S: Grease the peppers with olive oil and bake on the grill until the peel starts to peel freely. If you put the pepper in the oven then bake without saying as it is, about 30 minutes at

180 degrees. Peel the peppers and seeds and cut into longitudinal slices.

Cut the courgettes and eggplants into thin slices. (No thicker 0.5 cm) Fry in a frying pan or grease with oil put on a barbecue. They should be very soft.

Grease the tomatoes with oil and put on the barbecue. Or just fry in the same frying pan in which the eggplant was fried.

Finely chop the garlic and mint. Mix with all the other ingredients for dressing.

Stir the vegetables on a platter and pour the dressing. Put the baked tomatoes on top.

The salad is good both warm and cold. It will serve as a great side dish for meat or fish.

Courgettes in the oven

Ingredients

1 Courgette

2 tbsp Olive oil

0.5 tsp Seasoning of grilled vegetables

1 clove Garlic

80 grams Cheese

Preparation

Cut the courgette into circles, add oil, seasoning, garlic through a press or a small grater.

Put on a baking tray (covered with parchment) courgettes at 220 C for 25 minutes. Then take out of the oven sprinkled with cheese and again for 5 minutes.

Enjoy your meal!

Mashed potatoes with onionsand grilled sausages

1h05

Ingredients

4 Sausages

Salt

Pepper and nutmeg

3 tbsp Freshly grated parmesan

5 tbsp Olive oil

1 kg Potato

400 g Onion

1 Egg

Preparation

Total time: 1h05

Preparation: 40 mins

Cooking: 25 mins

STEP 1

Cook the potatoes, peeled and cut into small pieces in boiling salted water, for about 15 min, until tender.

STEP 2

At the same time, brown the peeled and finely chopped onions in a large pan containing olive oil, until they become transparent and lightly golden.

STEP 3

Drain the potatoes, mash them with a potato masher, add the beaten egg to them, stirring vigorously.

STEP 4

Join the onions with all their cooking oil, salt, pepper and nutmeg.

STEP 5

Tamp the puree in an oven dish, sprinkle it with grated Parmesan and brown in a very hot oven (preheated at a thermostat of 7/210 ° C).

STEP 6

Serve hot, with grilled sausages and a salad.

Kobe beef tataki, grilled flaxseed condiment, carrotmousseline with ginger

40 mins

Ingredients

400 g Kobe beef

20 g Miso (fermented rice paste)

1 Lime

1 clove

Pink garlic

5 cl Mirin

1 kg Early carrot with its tops

10 g Ginger

100 g Butter

30 cl Soya sauce

30 g Fir honey

2 Spring onions

1 stick

Lemongrass

Preparation

Total time: 40 mins

Preparation: 20 mins

Cooking: 20 mins

STEP 1

Marinade: mix, garlic, miso paste, lime juice, mirin, 5 cl of soy sauce.

STEP 2

Cut the beef into 5 cm sections.

STEP 3

Marinate for 1 hour.

STEP 4

Soy reduction: halve the soy sauce with the finely chopped lemongrass and honey then strain through cheesecloth. Cut the scallion finely and add to this reduction, set aside at room temperature.

STEP 5

Carrot mousseline: peel the carrots, cut into slices, cook in the English style, they must be tender. Mix everything very smooth, and whip up with the butter and finish with the fresh ginger grated with a micro-plane, adjust the seasoning.

STEP 6

Grilled flaxseed condiment: dry roast the flax seeds then mix while hot with linseed oil, season.

STEP 7

Snack the beef in olive oil on each side and cut into ½ cm slices.

STEP 8

Dressage:

STEP 9

Place the carrot mousseline at the bottom of the plate.

STEP 10

Add the meat to the bottom of the plate like a carpaccio but in line.

STEP 11

Make dots of condiments around then sprinkle generously with the soya reduction on the meat.

STEP 12

Optional: fry the carrot tops and place a few sprigs on the plate.

STEP 13

Enjoy your meal!

Grilled salmon steak with honey and pink berries

25 mins

Ingredients

Salt

Pepper

Olive oil1 tbsp

Mustard

2 pods Garlic

3 tbsp Honey

2 pavers Salmon

1 tbsp Crushed pink berries

1 Onion

Preparation

Total time: 25 mins

Preparation: 10 minutes

Cooking: 15 mins

STEP 1

Prepare a sauce with honey, mustard, pink berries and 3 tablespoons of olive oil

STEP 2

Coat the fish and allow it marinate for 1 hour

STEP 3

Peel and chop garlic and onion.

STEP 4

In a sauté pan, heat 2 tablespoons of olive oil then brown the garlic and onion for 5 minutes.

STEP 5

Add the salmon steaks starting with the skin side and cook 10 to 15 minutes depending on the thickness of the steaks.

Grilled chicken breasts withyogurt and cucumbers

35 mins

Ingredients

Salt

Pepper

1 tbsp Olive oil

1 Tomato

2 Free-range chicken breasts (skinless)

2 Limes

3 Plain yogurts

½ Cucumber

2 Fresh onions

Total time: 35 mins

Preparation: 15 mins

Cooking: 20 mins

Preparation

Make several fairly deep and parallel notches, about 2 cm apart, in the flesh of the chicken breasts.

In a salad bowl, mix 2 yogurts with the juice of 1 lime and 1 tablespoon of olive oil; add salt and pepper.

Turn the chicken breasts several times in this sauce, then cover with plastic wrap.

Place in the fridge, the time to prepare the garnish.

Cut the cucumber in 2, lengthwise, remove the seeds, cut it into half-moons.

Cut the tomato, seed it, squeeze it and cut it into thin strips. Then cut the onions into small cubes.

Drain the chicken breasts, and then pat them dry with paper towels.

Cook them for 20 min under the grill of the oven, at 200 ° C (th 6-7); turn them halfway through cooking ... For the youngest, ask an adult for the oven!

Cut 1 lime into quarters, and grill it for 2 minutes per side. Present the raw vegetables, with the grilled chicken breasts and the salted and peppered yogurt in a bowl.

Grilled chickpeas

1h05

Ingredients

Pepper

1 teaspoon Salt

2 tbsp Olive oil

2 pods Garlic

1 pinch Bicarbonate

200 g Dried or canned chickpeas

Preparation

Total time: 1h05

Preparation: 5 min

Cooking: 1 hour

Soak the chickpeas for like 12 hours in water with a pinch of baking soda.

Baking soda is to alleviate the effects of chickpeas during digestion, if you know what I mean!

Drain the chickpeas, then cook them for 1 hour 30 minutes in a large saucepan of boiling water.

In a salad bowl, pour olive oil, minced garlic, salt and a few turns of the pepper mill.

Drain the chickpeas, and pour them into the salad bowl.

Mix well, so that the peas are all covered with the mixture.

Cover the oven rack using an aluminum foil, and pour in the seasoned chickpeas. Be careful, they must be well spread and not overlap!

Cook on the grill for 10 minutes. The chickpeas are ready when they are no longer soft. They must be very crunchy, but especially not blackened!

Let cool, and serve as an aperitif. The chickpeas will keep for a long time in an airtight container.

Grilled vegetables in the oven

Ingredients

150g courgette 50g onion

100g Bell pepper

100g carrots

150g mushrooms

On the marinade:

4 tbsp vegetable oil

1 tbsp soy sauce

1 tbsp apple cider vinegar

1 tsp liquid honey

1 tsp paprika

2 cloves garlic

to taste salt, spices

Preparation

Prepare the marinade.

Finely chop the garlic. Combine all the ingredients of the marinade, mix well.

Prepare vegetables and mushrooms.

Courgettes and mushrooms clean from the skin. Cut the vegetables arbitrarily.

Then turn over the vegetables dip in the marinade, put on a plate to make an extra marinade stack.

Mushrooms grease with a brush, otherwise they will take in excess marinade (mushrooms like a sponge absorb liquid). Then spread on the grill, covered with parchment.

Bake in the oven at t 250 degrees for about 15 minutes. Who wants to fry harder, time to add.

Vegetables ready!

Grilled vegetables are well suited as a side dish for meat and fish dishes, as well as as an independent dish.

Grilled trout on the barbecue

32 min

Ingredients

6 Trout Handled butter
12 slices Bacon

Preparation

Total time: 32 min
Preparation: 20 mins
Cooking: 12 mins

After having cleaned the trout well, fill their stomachs with the handled butter (personally, I take a snail butter, but any other herbs can be suitable according to your taste).

Cover each side of the trout with the slices of bacon and hold them with a kitchen string (two people for this operation helps a lot).

Cook them 6 minutes per side with a barbecue.

The bacon will have protected the trout from any burning and the butter will have given an incomparable softness.

Mediterranean grilledmackerel

25 mins

Ingredients

1 bouquet

Parsley

Salt

Pepper

2 tbsp Olive oil

1 Lemon

4 Mackerel

Preparation

Total time: 25 mins

Preparation: 15 mins

Cooking: 10 minutes

STEP 1

Empty the mackerel and grill them on the barbecue or under the broiler (about 10-15 minutes).

STEP 2

Chop the parsley, mix it with lemon juice and oil.

STEP 3

Season with salt and pepper. Drizzle each mackerel with this sauce before serving.

Grilled sea bass with herbs

36 mins

Ingredients

Freshly ground black pepper

50 g Coarse gray salt from Guérande

1 teaspoon Olive oil

1/2 bunch Flat parsley

1 Bar (or a wolf) of 1.3 kg or 2 bars of 800 g each

2 strands Fennel or 1 pinch of fennel seeds

Preparation

Total time: 36 mins

Preparation: 20 mins

Cooking: 16 mins

STEP 1

Without scaling or washing it, cut the fins and gut the fish.

STEP 2

Mix the coarse salt with the herbs and pepper. Garnish the inside of the fish and close with wooden skewers.

STEP 3

Let the fish rest in a cool place for at least 30 minutes so that the herbs smell and perfume it. Wrap the thin part of the tail in foil.

STEP 4

Preheat your grill or barbecue, oil the grill and cook the fish for 9 minutes on one side then for 7 minutes on the other.

STEP 5

Check the cooking by pulling on the dorsal ridge, near the head, which should come without resisting.

STEP 6

Put the sea bass on a cutting board and remove the heat hardened skin. Sprinkle with salt and pepper. Serve whole on a heated dish with olive oil or a sauce of your choice.

STEP 7

If you don't have a grill, cook the fish for 20 minutes in an oven preheated to 200 ° C (thermostat 6-7).

Grilled sea bream fillets with mustard and shallots

30 mins

Ingredients

Salt

Pepper

1 tbsp Mustard

5 cl White wine

2 fillets Dorade royal

5 Shallots

4 Bay leaves

30 g Butter

Preparation

Total time: 30 mins

Preparation: 15 mins

Cooking: 15 mins

STEP 1

Preheat the oven on the grill position.

STEP 2

Peel and finely chop the shallots. Spread them out into the bottom of a gratin dish, add the bay leaf and cover with the white wine.

STEP 3

Place the sea bream fillets on the bed of shallots. Spread them with mustard. Season with salt and pepper and sprinkle with shavings of butter.

STEP 4

Grill the sea bream for 15 to 20 min.

Grilled Pepper Cake in Oil

1h15

Ingredients

Pepper

Salt

Provence herbs

15 cl Milk

10 cl Oil (oil from peppers)

1 jar Grilled peppers in oil

1 bag Yeast

250 g Flour

4 Eggs

100 g Grated cheese

Preparation

Total time: 1h15

Preparation: 15 mins

Cooking: 1 hour

STEP 1

Combine the oil, eggs, milk, salt, pepper and Provence herbs.

STEP 2

Add the flour and baking powder.

STEP 3

Add the Gruyere, the peppers cut into small strips.

STEP 4

Mix well, pour the preparation into a cake mold.

STEP 5

Bake for 1 hour at 180 ° C.